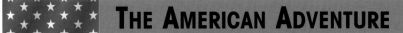 

CATTLE TRAILS AND COWBOYS

SALLY SENZELL ISAACS

Heinemann Library
Chicago, Illinois

© 2004 Heinemann Library
a division of Reed Elsevier Inc.
Chicago, Illinois

Customer Service 888-454-2279

Visit our website at www.heinemannlibrary.com

Produced for Heinemann Library by
   Bender Richardson White.
Editor: Lionel Bender
Designer and Page Makeup: Ben White
Picture Researcher: Cathy Stastny
Production Controller: Kim Richardson

07 06 05 04 03
10 9 8 7 6 5 4 3 2 1

Printed in China, by WKT Company Limited

Library of Congress Cataloging-in-Publication Data

Isaacs, Sally Senzell, 1950-
   Cattle trails and cowboys / Sally Senzell Isaacs.
      v. cm. – (The American adventure)
   Includes bibliographical references and index.
   Contents: Texas cattle country – A new way to make money –
   Year-round at the ranch – The cowboy – The Chisholm trail –
   Life on the trail – Cowboys: keep out – The cow town – The
   wild west – A deadly winter – End of the cowboy days –
   Historical map of the United States.
   ISBN 1-4034-2502-7 (HC library binding)
   ISBN 1-4034-4773-X (PB)
   1. Cowboys–Texas–History–19th century–Juvenile literature.
   2. Cowboys–Oklahoma–History–19th century–Juvenile
   literature. 3. Ranch life-Texas-History–19th century–Juvenile
   literature. 4. Ranch life–Oklahoma–History–19th century–
   Juvenile literature. 5. Cattle trails-Texas-History–19th
   century–Juvenile literature. 6. Cattle trails–Oklahoma–History–
   19th century–Juvenile literature. 7. Texas–History–1846-1950-
   -Juvenile literature. 8. Oklahoma–History–19th century–
   Juvenile literature. [1. Cowboys–History–19th century. 2.
   Ranch life-Texas-History–19th century. 3. Ranch life–
   Oklahoma–History–19th century. 4. Cattle trails. 5. Texas–
   History–1846-1950. 6. Oklahoma–History–19th century.] I.
   Title.
   F391.I83 2004
   976.4'05-dc22
                                                 2003013021

Special thanks to Mike Carpenter and Geof Knight at Heinemann
Library for editorial and design guidance and direction.

Acknowledgments
The producers and publishers are grateful to the following for
permission to reproduce copyright material:
Bettmann/Corbis Images, page 19. Peter Newark's American
Pictures, pages 6, 9, 12, 14, 16, 20, 23, 25, 26.

Illustrations by John James
Maps by Stefan Chabluk
Cover art by John James

Every effort has been made to contact copyright holders of any
material reproduced in this book. Omissions will be rectified in
subsequent printings if notice is given to the publisher.

QUOTATIONS
The quotations in this book come from *We Pointed
Them West—Recollections of a Cowpuncher* by
E.C. Abbott and Helena Huntington Smith.
University of Oklahoma Press, 1939.

The Author
Sally Senzell Isaacs is a professional writer and
editor of nonfiction books for children. She
graduated from Indiana University, earning a B.S.
degree in education with majors in American
history and sociology. She is the author of the nine
titles in the *America in the Time of...* series
published by Heinemann Library and of the first
sixteen titles in Heinemann Library's *Picture the
Past* series. Sally Senzell Isaacs lives in New
Jersey with her husband and two children.

The Consultant
Our thanks to William D. Welge, CA, director
Research Division, Oklahoma Historical Society, for
his comments in the preparation of this book.

ABOUT THIS BOOK

This book is about America in the time of the cowboys and the great cattle drives out of Texas. The term *America* means the United States of America (also called the U.S.) The book focuses on the years 1840 to 1890 because these were the most active years for cowboys. Actually, cowboys and their work started in the 1500s in Mexico, when settlers from Spain began bringing cattle there.

The Spaniards trained the local American Indians to become vaqueros—workers who took care of the cattle. Later, Texas cowboys learned how to do their job from the vaqueros. *Cowboy* is the term used for a person who took care of cattle on ranches and on the trails. All of this took place in the "Wild West," the nickname for the wide-open spaces and free-spirited towns of the West and Southwest.

CONTENTS

ABOUT THE SERIES

The American Adventure is a series of books about important events that shaped the United States of America. Each book focuses on one event. While learning about the event, the reader will also learn how the people and places of the time influenced the nation's future. The little illustrations at the top left of each two-page article are a symbol of the times. They are identified in the Contents on page 3.

▼ This map shows the United States today, with the borders and names of all the states. Refer to this map, or to the one on pages 28 and 29, to locate places talked about in this book.

AMERICA'S STORY

Throughout the book, the yellow panels, showing a cowboy's hat, gloves, and stirrups, contain information that tells the more general history of the United States of America.

THE FEATURE STORY

The green panels, showing a cowboy on horseback, contain more detailed information about the cowboy's life and the cattle trails, this book's feature event.

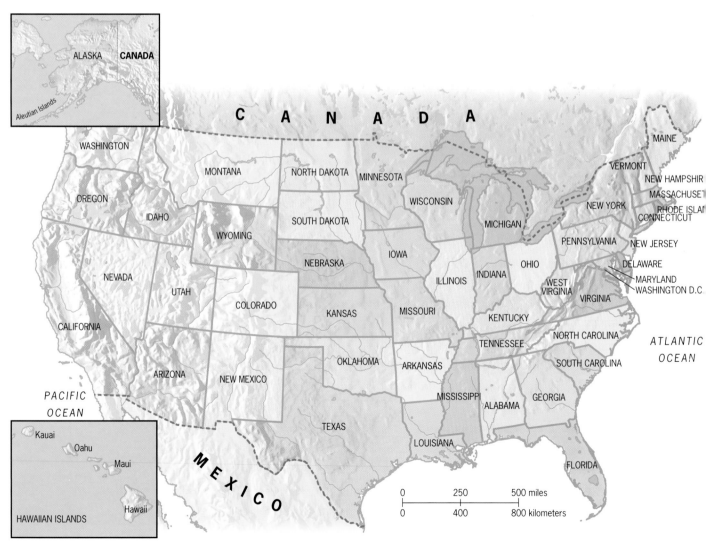

CATTLE TRAILS AND COWBOYS: INTRODUCTION

Thanks to movies, television, and books, just about everyone knows what a cowboy is. People know him by his horse, hat, vest, and boots. They know him by his tough, brave personality and his action-packed life. But this is not a total picture of the cowboy. This book explores the everyday life of a cowboy. Real cowboys had to be tough and brave, but their lives were not always action-packed. In fact, there was a great deal of hard, dirty work and boredom. Movies and television usually show cowboys as white men. In real life, many cowboys were Mexican, African American, and American Indian. Another term for cowboys is cowhand. There were some female cowhands, but not many. In those days, people thought that the work of a cowboy was much too rough for women.

The history of the western cowboy grew out of the history of cattle farming in Texas. There was a time in the 1800s when thousands of cows and bulls wandered freely across the Texas plains. At first, most of the cattle belonged to no one. Anyone could take them, if they could wrestle a wild animal that weighed nearly 1,000 pounds (450 kilograms). In the 1860s, gathering cattle and selling them for beef became big business. The owners of those businesses were called ranchers. They hired thousands of workers—called cowboys—to capture the cattle, take care of them, and get them to a place where people were willing to pay a lot of money for them.

Cowboys followed miles and miles of trail, as they walked huge herds of cattle from ranches in Texas to towns with railroads in Kansas, Wyoming, and other places. There were several trails leading to the railroad towns. The most famous went from San Antonio, Texas, to Abilene, Kansas. It has been called by many names, including the Trail, the Kansas Trail, and the Texas–Abilene Trail. Its most famous name is the Chisholm Trail. In fact, the original Chisholm Trail started in Oklahoma, not Texas, but today people use the name for the entire trail.

TEXAS CATTLE COUNTRY

Today cattle (cows and steers) are important because they provide beef for our dinner tables. But the beef business was not important until the 1860s, after refrigeration methods were improved. Before then, people valued cattle as a source for leather, candles, and soap.

About 500 years ago, settlers from Spain moved to Mexico and brought their horses and cattle with them. North America offered plenty of land for the animals to roam freely. Ranchers, the people who lived on the land, needed help looking after the cattle herds. They taught the local Mexican Indians how to ride horses and catch the wild cattle. The Indians became skilled at their jobs. They were called vaqueros.

By the early 1700s, Spanish people were moving from Mexico up to present-day Texas. They brought their cattle with them and started new ranches. Many vaqueros came with them. The vaqueros rounded up cattle and killed some when they needed food. They also stripped the hides, and made them into leather boots and saddles. They used fat from the animals, called tallow, to make candles and soap.

By 1850, 330,000 wild cattle roamed through Texas. Just like deer and buffalo, the cattle had no owners. They were available to anyone who needed them and could catch them. This was not an easy job. One witness described the cattle as "fifty times more dangerous to footmen than the fiercest buffalo."

From vaqueros to cowboys
Some Texas ranchers saw a chance to make money by gathering cattle and selling them. During the California gold rush (1849 to 1854), ranchers paid vaqueros to walk the cattle from Texas to California, where they were sold for beef. In Texas, cattle cost between $5 and $15 apiece. In California, people were willing to pay up to $100. By this time, the vaqueros were teaching their skills to American Indians, African Americans, and white men who worked for the Texas ranchers. U.S. citizens started calling these workers *cowboys*.

▼ James Walker painted this picture of a Spanish vaquero. He has caught the steer by wrapping a rope around its neck and front legs. In Spanish, the rope is called *la reata*. American cowboys called it a lariat.

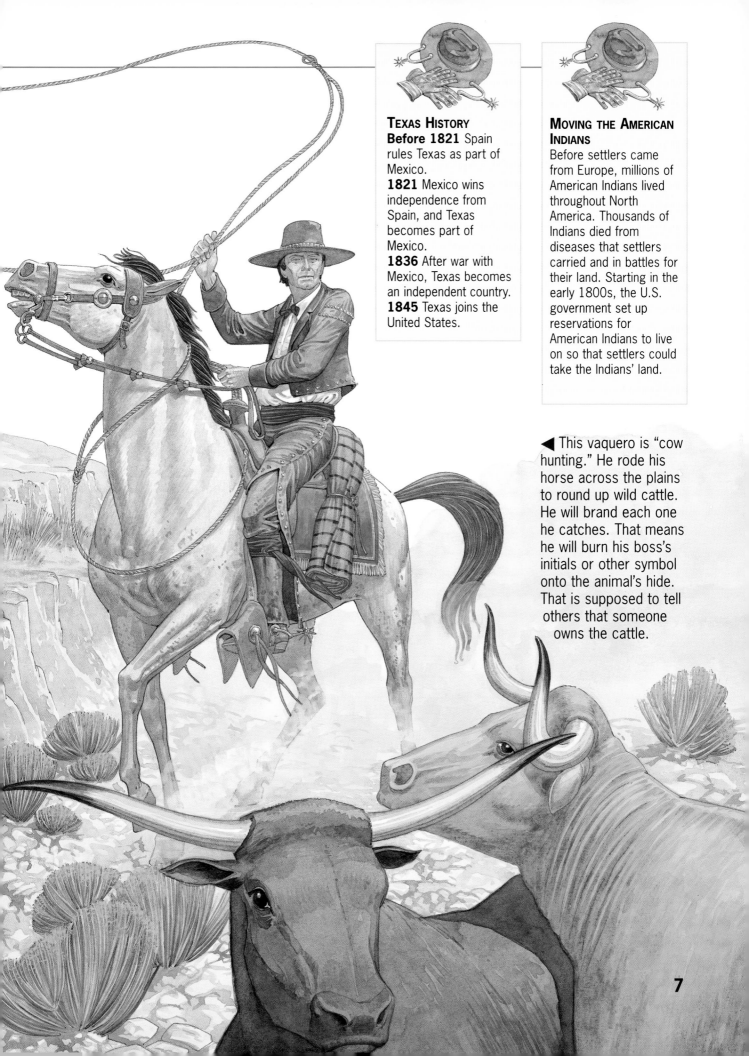

TEXAS HISTORY
Before 1821 Spain rules Texas as part of Mexico.
1821 Mexico wins independence from Spain, and Texas becomes part of Mexico.
1836 After war with Mexico, Texas becomes an independent country.
1845 Texas joins the United States.

MOVING THE AMERICAN INDIANS
Before settlers came from Europe, millions of American Indians lived throughout North America. Thousands of Indians died from diseases that settlers carried and in battles for their land. Starting in the early 1800s, the U.S. government set up reservations for American Indians to live on so that settlers could take the Indians' land.

◄ This vaquero is "cow hunting." He rode his horse across the plains to round up wild cattle. He will brand each one he catches. That means he will burn his boss's initials or other symbol onto the animal's hide. That is supposed to tell others that someone owns the cattle.

7

CATTLE, JOBS, AND MONEY

The nation's states fought one another in the Civil War from 1861 to 1865. Six hundred thousand U.S. citizens died in the war. More than 50,000 Texan soldiers fought for the South. When the South lost the war, Texas soldiers came home to tough times.

THE COMANCHE
The Comanche had lived in Texas for hundreds of years. Then Texans took over the land. As the cattle drives tramped through their land, the Comanche attacked them. The U.S. government sent soldiers to fight the Comanche. In 1867, the Comanche agreed to move to Indian Territory.

Before the Civil War, some ranchers had made money by taking their cattle to cities and towns in the North. During the war, President Abraham Lincoln stopped people in the northern states from buying southern products. The southern states formed their own country and made their own money. When they lost the war, their money had no value, and nearly everyone was poor. The only thing Texas had plenty of was cattle. By 1865, there were over six million wild cattle in Texas.

There was a demand for cattle in the North. People in towns and cities such as Chicago, Boston, and New York liked beef and were willing to pay a high price for it. There was also a demand for beef to feed workers on the new railroads across the Great Plains, American Indians living on the western reservations, and gold miners in Denver, Colorado.

As a result, big cattle drives began. Cattle ranchers hired cowboys to round up wild cattle and walk them across deserts, rivers, and Indian Territory. Many young soldiers from Texas and other southern states were happy to get jobs as cowboys. Some were former African American slaves who were freed after the Civil War.

▼ In 1866, Oliver Loving and Charles Goodnight led 2,000 cattle to the Denver gold mines. They passed a reservation at Fort Sumner, New Mexico, where the U.S. Army was trying to take care of 8,500 starving Navajo Indians. The army bought $12,000 in cattle and ordered more. The trail from Texas to Colorado was named the Goodnight–Loving Trail.

8

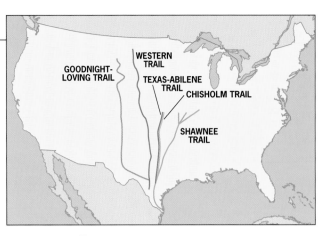

This is a Texas longhorn. The first longhorns came from Mexico. They were strong but had little meat. Ranchers decided to breed them with meatier cattle brought in by U.S. settlers. The new Texas longhorn was well suited for the long cattle drives. These strong, long-legged animals could walk great distances without tiring and go without water for long periods.

STAMPEDE FOR WATER
When cattle got thirsty, they became wild. One time on the Goodnight–Loving Trail, 2,000 thirsty animals smelled water. They stampeded, shoving each other over cliffs into the river. More than 100 were drowned or trampled to death.

The cattle drives followed trails first used by American Indians, traders, and settlers. The cattle could walk all the way to the western reservations and gold mines, but eastern cities were too far away. So, they walked to towns that had railroads. From there, the cattle rode trains to the East.

YEAR-ROUND AT THE RANCH

By 1867, the cattle business was growing strong. Cattle had become something to own. They were possessions, like horses. Many Texas ranchers gathered thousands of cattle, branded them, and sold them for high profit. A ranch was like a smooth-running business or factory.

Each spring and fall, there was a roundup. Because ranches had no fences, cattle roamed miles away from the ranch center. Cattle from several ranches mingled together. For the roundup, groups of cowboys spread out in all directions looking for their boss's cattle. By whistling and shouting at the animals, each cowboy made many of them move in one direction. Slowly, he gathered a large herd and moved it toward a roundup area.

At the roundup area, the cowboys sorted out the cattle. They looked for a certain clipping on the cattle's ears, or for the owner's brand—symbol—marked on the animals' hides. If an animal had no brand, the cowboy branded it for his boss. New calves were branded at this time, too. The roundup could last several weeks.

STOPPING RUSTLERS
Cowboys were always on the lookout for rustlers. These were thieves who stole cattle that did not belong to them. After taking an animal, the rustler burned lines and circles over the brand so that the owner would not recognize it. Cowboys carried brand books that showed the brands of different owners. Ranchers printed their brands in newspapers to help identification.

◀ Branding the calves was a dusty, noisy process. In the roundup area, the cowboys built a fire and heated up the branding iron. One cowboy rode near a calf, tossed a lariat over its head, and dragged it near the fire. Another cowboy pinned the calf to the ground while two others pressed the iron onto its skin. Sometimes a fourth cowboy would cut a notch in the animal's ear. After this was done, the calf scrambled to its feet and ran off to find its mother.

Winter jobs—or out of work

Some cowboys stayed on the ranch during the winter months, getting ready for the next roundup. They mended saddles, put shoes on the horses, and fixed their ropes. They also took turns riding horses through snow and ice to check the cattle on the range. Many cowboys had no job in the winter. Without a home or paycheck, they traveled from ranch to ranch looking for odd jobs, such as house painting.

▲ This "broncobuster" takes horses that have never been ridden and gets them used to a saddle and rider. It could take six days to "break" the horse's wild spirit. There were many other jobs on the ranch. The foreman was in charge of all the workers. A cook prepared the food. Wranglers took care of the horses. Behind this broncobuster is a building called the bunkhouse. Cowboys slept there.

RANCH BRANDS
Each ranch had its own branding symbol. Here are some:

A K
T ♀

THE TYPICAL COWBOY

Most cowboys were under 30 years old. Many were even teenagers. Most were poor and worked 7 days a week, 17 hours a day, for about a dollar a day—about 12 dollars in today's money.

These young men were not ordinary fellows who could be happy selling hats in a store or planting wheat on a farm. They were looking for adventure. They came from different places. Some were even running away from the law. During the busy season, cattle ranchers were happy to have them, and did not ask questions about their pasts. Some cowboys stayed for just one exhausting cattle drive. Few stayed more than seven years.

The cowboy's work could be boring, lonely, difficult, and dangerous. Many cowboys died from accidents, freezing weather, and cattle stampedes. On the ranch, the day started before sunrise. The bunkhouse, where the cowboys slept, was cold in the winter, hot in the summer, and usually had countless bedbugs. Big ranches had a mess hall. Cowboys usually ate silently and quickly since work was always waiting. Some spent their day riding the range alone, looking for stray cattle or helping ones that were injured or stuck in the mud.

Leisure-time activities

Evenings on the ranch were spent quietly. The cowboys stayed in the bunkhouse, reading books, looking through mail-order catalogs, or writing letters home. Some sat by the fireplace playing cards.

Sometimes cowboys got a day off from the ranch. They enjoyed hunting for wild turkeys or deer. They also held their own competitions in broncobusting, horse racing, or calf roping. These contests eventually grew into rodeos, organized competitions to show off cowboy skills.

BUFFALO
From 1872 to 1876, non-Indian hunters killed four million buffalo on the Great Plains. They sold the meat to railroad companies to feed the workers. Bones were sold to factories in the East. The Kiowa, Comanche, Arapaho, and Cheyenne people could not survive without the buffalo. They tried to fight the hunters, but then were forced to move to reservations. Cattle ranchers and farmers took over the land of the buffalo and the Plains Indians.

▼ This cowboy has everything he needs on his saddle or in his deep vest pockets. He has an oilskin raincoat tied behind him and a rifle under his leg. Most cowboys did not carry a rifle.

▼ The cowboy's hat kept the sun out of his eyes and the rain off his neck. The cloth, called a bandana, kept the sun off his neck, but also could be pulled over his nose and mouth to keep out the dust. To protect his legs from thorns and cactus, he wore leather or wool chaps over his pants.

▼ Every cowboy needed a sturdy lariat. He usually caught an animal with the "overhead swing" over the animal's horns or head. He could also toss a "heeling catch" under an animal's back feet. Ropes were also used to pull a cow out of the mud or drag firewood to the ranch.

NAT LOVE
Nat Love was born an African American slave in Tennessee in 1854. In 1869, after the Civil War, he headed for Kansas and the life of a cowboy. For 20 years, he worked on cattle drives. In Deadwood, South Dakota, he won contests in shooting, riding, and roping. He became known by his nickname, Deadwood Dick.

THE CHISHOLM TRAIL

A man named Joseph McCoy is given credit for building the cattle business. In 1867, he persuaded the Kansas Pacific Railroad to create a train stop at the tiny town of Abilene, Kansas. There he built a hotel, bank, and fenced-in areas to hold 3,000 cattle.

Joseph McCoy found a trail that would give cowboys the fewest rivers, hills, towns, farms, and Indian land to cross. He told Texas cattle owners to send their cattle up to the Red River at the border of Texas and the Indian Territory (present-day Oklahoma). From there, they should follow the wagon tracks made by Jesse Chisholm, a trader who took goods back and forth from Indian camps to his stores in Kansas. In time, the trail from San Antonio, Texas, to Abilene, Kansas, became known as the Chisholm Trail.

ADVERTISING THE TRAIL
Joseph McCoy sent advertisements to Texas. One ad boasted about the Chisholm Trail. "It is more direct. It has more prairies, less timber, more small streams and fewer large ones, altogether better grass and fewer flies—no civilized Indian tax or wild Indian disturbances —than any other route yet driven over."

TEXAS FEVER
Cattle drives were not allowed through Missouri. Texas cattle carried ticks that caused Texas fever. Longhorns did not get sick, but the weaker cows in other states died from the fever. Missouri farmers stopped the cattle drives at their border. Then they passed laws against them. Kansas passed similar laws. Later, cattle drives were allowed in Kansas when Joseph McCoy promised to pay farmers for any losses.

▲Charles Goodnight invented a new type of chuckwagon with a swing-down table and storage drawers and boxes. It also had a large water barrel attached to one side.

The cattle drive

More than 35,000 cattle arrived in Abilene that first year. Thousands more followed. For three to four months, cattle and cowboys rode the dusty trails to Kansas. A trail boss was in charge of each cattle drive. He chose 10 to 15 cowboys to handle between 2,000 and 3,000 cattle. No one knew what surprises waited on the trail. Sudden noises, such as thunder or even a loud sneeze, could startle the cattle and cause a crushing stampede. The panicked animals could knock cowboys off their horses and trample them. After a stampede, it sometimes took a week to find all the cattle.

▼ On the trail, the herd was brought to a stop at the end of each day.

1. *Point riders* rode in front of the herd. They set the pace and kept the cattle heading in the right direction.

2. *Swing riders* rode beside the herd and made sure the cattle did not spread out too far.

3. *Flank riders* rode behind the swing riders, watching for stray cattle.

4. *Wranglers* were in charge of the extra riding horses. Cowboys switched horses three or four times a day.

5. The *drag riders* rode at the back of the herd, watching for stray and slow cattle in the rear.

6. The *cook* drove the mule-drawn chuckwagon and prepared meals for the cowboys.

LIFE ON THE TRAIL

"I'm up in the mornin' afore daylight. And afore I sleep the moon shines bright. No chaps and no slicker, and it's pouring down rain. And I swear, by God, that I'll never night-herd again." These are words from a cowboy song called "The Old Chisholm Trail."

HEADING NORTH
Before going to sleep at night, the cook would turn the chuckwagon to face the North Star. In the morning, he and the trail boss were sure to head the cattle drive north to Kansas.

Cowboys sang and whistled as they rode along the trail. They made up tunes to the beat of the horses' hooves. A cowboy's job was to keep the cattle quiet and calm through the long days and nights. Longhorns were jittery animals and almost anything—a duck, rattlesnake, thunderstorm, or bright lantern—could scare them and start them stampeding in all directions.

The trail day started before sunrise when the cook woke up to prepare biscuits, bacon, and coffee. The cowboys tied up their bedrolls, tossed them on the chuckwagon, and grabbed their breakfast. The cook packed up the chuckwagon and headed off with the trail boss to find the next source of water and grass for the cattle. The cowboys and animals followed behind. They stopped at noon to rest and eat.

On the journey north from Texas, there were at least six rivers to cross, and some were deep and muddy. Animals got caught in quicksand or in branches that fell from trees along the river. If the animals struggled, they could push each other under the water and drown. Charles Goodnight once said a big herd in the river "looked like a million floating rocking chairs."

▼The artist W. R. Leigh painted this picture in 1912. It shows the danger faced by cowboys during a stampede.

Nighttime

The cowboys tried to keep the cattle walking at a steady pace. If they walked too fast, the cattle might lose weight, making them less valuable. The group stopped for dinner when they saw the chuckwagon parked for the night. At night the cowboys rode around the herd, pushing it into a tighter circle around the wagon. They then took turns riding around the circle, singing softly to the animals.

▲ At night, cowboys and cattle slept near the chuckwagon. Cattle usually slept on the ground, but this herd has been startled to its feet by a bolt of lightning. The cowboys have heard the cattle stirring and will try to calm the animals down so that they do not run away.

PAYDAY
When he sold the cattle in Kansas, the trail boss took the money and paid the other cowboys. Here is what they made and what that money is worth today:

- Trail boss: $100 a month ($1,765)
- Cook: $35–$50 a month ($617–$885)
- Wrangler: $25 a month ($441)
- Other cowboys: $30 a month ($529)

COWBOYS: KEEP OUT

To get from San Antonio to Abilene was a journey of about 1,000 miles (1,600 kilometers). The cattle drives crossed Indian Territory and Kansas farmland. Both the American Indians and the farmers tried hard to keep the cattle off their land.

▼ The cattle have crossed the deadline and are at the front door of the farm. The family is warning the trail boss to keep the cattle away. One cowboy, Teddy Blue Abbott, described the cowboys' point of view. He said the farmers "would plant a crop alongside the trail and … then when the cattle got into their wheat or their garden patch, they would come cussing and waving a shotgun and yelling for damages."

Kit Carson, Jr., the Crack Shot of the West.

A WILD LIFE ROMANCE, BY "BUCKSKIN SAM."

▲ These books were called dime novels, though many cost just a nickel. More than 2,000 were printed, all of them action-packed and starring cowboys as brave heroes. U.S. citizens loved the stories and had no idea that a cowboy's life was often boring.

THE RAILROAD
By 1880, railroad workers had laid 93,000 miles (148,800 kilometers) of railroad tracks across the United States. Millions of U.S. citizens and people from other countries were settling on farms and ranches across the Great Plains. The railroads transported the settlers and the goods they needed. Railroads eventually came to Texas to take cattle north. This ended the cowboy's job.

PICTURE AMERICA
In 1876, the United States was 100 years old. Imagine a vertical line through the nation that splits Kansas in half. To the east of the line, 42 million people lived in 31 states. To the west, 2 million people were spread over 7 states and 9 territories. But people were moving west quickly. In 1870, the population of Kansas was 364,339. By 1890, it was 1,428,108— almost four times larger.

Indian Territory
The U.S. government promised to take care of the American Indians on reservations in Indian Territory, but these promises were broken. The Indians struggled to survive. Some tried to raise their own cattle and grow food. They did not want thousands of cattle traveling over their land. Some tribes demanded that the trail boss pay a toll, a fee for passing through. Sometimes angry tribes tried to cause a stampede by waving blankets or firing guns at the cattle. During the confusion, they tried to catch cattle for food.

Settlers
As the buffalo disappeared from the plains, settlers and ranchers began moving to Kansas. These people, too, hated the cattle drives. They raised their own animals, and the traveling cattle were eating the good grass as well as their crops. Settlers also feared that their animals would catch Texas fever, a disease carried by ticks on the cattle. Farmers marked the borders of their farms with "deadlines." If a cattle drive crossed the deadline, the farmers shot at them or at least threatened to.

Some people who lived along the trail became cattle rustlers. They started stampedes and caught cattle for themselves. Others pretended to be officers of the law and asked for cattle as payment for crossing a border. All this made the cowboys angry. Though a cowboy usually owned a gun, he rarely used it. Some trail bosses made cowboys keep their guns in the chuckwagon.

THE END OF THE TRAIL

After living three to four months on the trail with nothing but a muddy river for a bathtub, the cowboys brought the cattle into a cow town. They pushed the cattle into pens by the train tracks while the trail boss or rancher met with cattle dealers to make a sale.

A cow town was a town along the trail where the cowboys stopped to put cattle onto the railroad. The cowboys spent a few days there to wash, sleep on clean sheets, and have fun. Once the cattle were sold, the cowboys got paid.

Teddy Blue Abbott described how that felt. "[T]hey paid us off, and [I] bought some new clothes and had my picture taken …. I had a new white Stetson hat that I paid ten dollars for and new pants that cost twelve dollars, and a good shirt and fancy boots. Lord, I was proud of those clothes! … I thought that I was dressed right for the first time in my life."

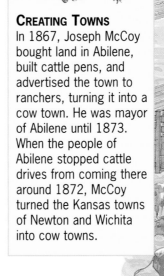

CREATING TOWNS
In 1867, Joseph McCoy bought land in Abilene, built cattle pens, and advertised the town to ranchers, turning it into a cow town. He was mayor of Abilene until 1873. When the people of Abilene stopped cattle drives from coming there around 1872, McCoy turned the Kansas towns of Newton and Wichita into cow towns.

▶ This is an advertisement to sell packaged beef and pork. Cowboys from Texas, Wyoming, Montana, and the Dakotas rounded up the cattle and put them on trains headed for cities such as Chicago and New York. There the animals were killed in slaughterhouses and packaged as beef for sale. A dealer might have bought cattle for $18 a head in Abilene and sold them for $30 or $40 a head in New York.

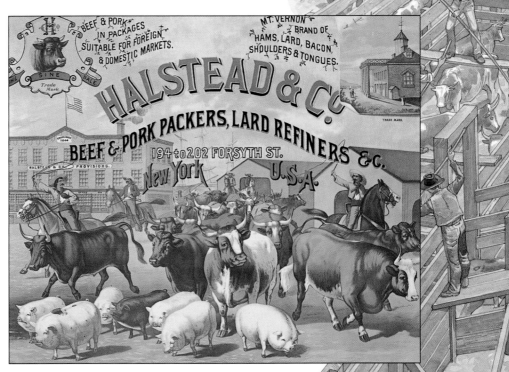

20

▼ The cowboys' last job on the cattle drive was to get the cattle counted, weighed, and onto the train. By 1871, Abilene received 700,000 cattle a year. After a few days of celebration, cowboys headed back to the ranch or to search for a winter job. Because they poked the cattle with poles, cowboys sometimes called themselves cowpokes or cowpunchers.

A GRAND HOTEL
Abilene had a fancy hotel called Drover's Cottage. The restaurant served roast beef and turkey, oyster pie, and fancy cake. Ranchers and other business owners sat on the wide porch and made their deals. When the cattle drives stopped coming and Abilene became just a regular farm town, the hotel was taken apart and shipped to Ellsworth, the next cow town.

Abilene, Kansas

After taking a hot bath and getting a haircut, the cowboys ran out to spend their money. Cowboy money helped these towns grow. For example, before it became a cow town, Abilene had one store. It served as the grocery store, clothing store, and post office. Then Joseph McCoy built some cattle pens, horse stables, and a three-story hotel.

By 1871, about 5,000 cowboys came off the Chisholm Trail at Abilene, and could sleep in ten boardinghouses or four hotels, drink liquor in 32 saloons, play cards at the 64 gambling tables, and buy anything from boots to diamonds in the five large stores. The people who lived in Abilene had two opinions of the wild cowboys. They were happy to get the money they spent. Yet, they did not like the shouting, shooting, and generally bad behavior of the cowboys.

21

THE WILD WEST

It was no wonder that the people of Abilene wanted to get rid of the cowboys. These citizens were trying to build their farms and raise their families. The cowboys, with their cursing, drinking, and gambling, set a bad example for children.

BELLE STARR
One of the few women outlaws of the Wild West was Myra Maybelle (Belle) Starr. She lived in Texas and spent most of her adult life with gangs of cattle thieves and horse thieves. When she was not in prison, she was running away from the law. She was shot to death in a fight in 1889.

STOP THE CATTLE
In 1872 the people in Abilene signed a statement and printed it in the *Abilene Chronicle*. The statement said, "...most respectfully request all who have contemplated driving Texas Cattle to Abilene the coming season to seek some other point for shipment, as the inhabitants of Dickinson (County) will no longer submit to the evils of the trade."

Most cowboys were not allowed to carry guns on the trail, but when they arrived in the cow town, they took them back. They would spend their time drinking in saloons and arguing at the card tables. Before long, they would start tumbling out the door with their guns drawn. Sometimes they would shoot the guns in the air just to make noise. Sometimes they would shoot in a deadly fight. Day and night, Abilene's main street was filled with loud music and shouting. Finally, the citizens demanded law and order.

Wild Bill Hickok
First, the citizens posted some laws in the newspaper and on signs. One of the laws forbade bringing guns into town. This hardly stopped the cowboys. They shot holes in the signs. The town leaders hired a marshal, someone to police the town. They picked James Butler Hickok, known by his nickname "Wild Bill."

Even the cowboys were afraid of Wild Bill. He was as wild as any cowboy and a sharpshooter as well. Hickok kept the peace for about eight months. Then he killed a man, perhaps accidentally, and the citizens sent him away. Soon after, they stopped the cattle drives from coming to town.

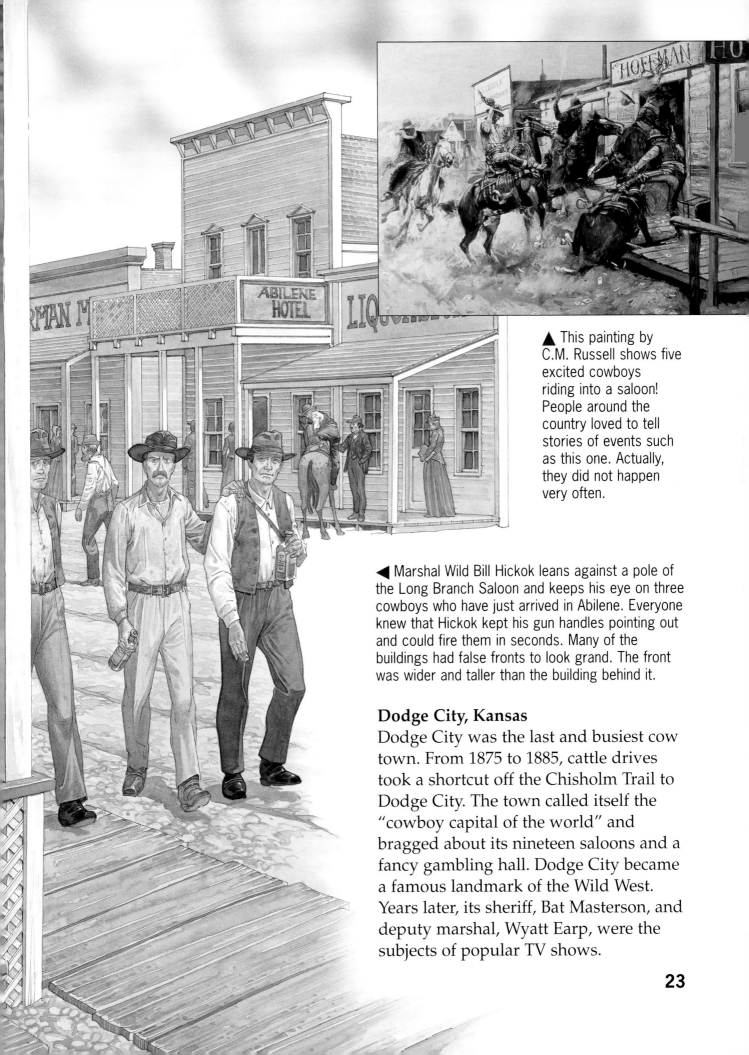

▲ This painting by C.M. Russell shows five excited cowboys riding into a saloon! People around the country loved to tell stories of events such as this one. Actually, they did not happen very often.

◄ Marshal Wild Bill Hickok leans against a pole of the Long Branch Saloon and keeps his eye on three cowboys who have just arrived in Abilene. Everyone knew that Hickok kept his gun handles pointing out and could fire them in seconds. Many of the buildings had false fronts to look grand. The front was wider and taller than the building behind it.

Dodge City, Kansas

Dodge City was the last and busiest cow town. From 1875 to 1885, cattle drives took a shortcut off the Chisholm Trail to Dodge City. The town called itself the "cowboy capital of the world" and bragged about its nineteen saloons and a fancy gambling hall. Dodge City became a famous landmark of the Wild West. Years later, its sheriff, Bat Masterson, and deputy marshal, Wyatt Earp, were the subjects of popular TV shows.

A DEADLY WINTER

Over the years, cattle ranching grew beyond Texas into Colorado, Wyoming, Montana, and the Dakotas. But by around 1884, there were too many cattle and not enough good grass for them to eat. Then nature dealt a terrible blow.

ONE BIG RANCH
In 1883, Mabel Doss Day owned the largest fenced ranch in Texas. At 78,000 acres (31,500 hectares), it was a little larger than the present-day city of Denver, Colorado.

First came three years with very little rain in 1884, 1885, and 1886. Grass withered on the range and on the trails. Creeks and streams dried up. Cattle became thinner than ever, but the ranchers rushed them to the cow towns before things got worse.

Then came the winter of 1886. First, an early snow left the grass covered with a layer of ice. Then, there were two fierce blizzards in December followed by a ten-day storm in January. In freezing temperatures, cowboys rode horses across the range, looking for animals caught in snowdrifts. They tried to lead the cattle to any place where the wind had blown the snow off the grass. They chopped up ice so the animals could drink. Despite the cowboys' efforts, hundreds of thousands of cattle died that winter. Many ranchers went out of business.

Barbed wire
Those ranchers who stayed in business made changes. They no longer wanted their cattle roaming across miles and miles of range. Using the newly invented barbed wire, ranchers fenced off their pastures and kept the cattle where they could be found easily. Ranchers also grew hay so they could feed the cattle throughout the winter.

▶ Two cowboys ride out to check on the cattle during a terrible blizzard. One cow has fallen into a snowdrift. Many others are dead, and the snow has piled up over their bodies. Those left standing turn their tails to the wind to try to protect themselves.
   On large ranches where cattle could roam miles away from the ranch buildings, cowboys slept in a one-room shack on the range. It was called the line camp. There was a fireplace and not much else.

A new breed
The price of the lean longhorns kept dropping. Ranchers decided to bring in meatier bulls and breed new kinds of cattle. The result was shorter cattle with higher-quality beef, such as Herefords, Durhams, and Brahmans. These animals could not walk long distances as the longhorns could. Cowboys had to dig watering ponds. They also built windmills to pump water from under the ground. These new breeds would not do well on the long cattle drives, but railroads were being built in Texas.

▶ Charles M. Russell painted this picture in 1887 after living through the deadly winter of 1886 in Montana. Russell moved to Montana at the age of 16. In 1882, he became a wrangler on a cattle drive. He loved to draw on the trail. After 11 years, he left the job, but he continued drawing and painting. His art became popular in New York City around 1911.

FENCE-CUTTING
After ranchers put up barbed-wire fences, a fence-cutting war began. Farmers and other ranchers often believed the fences blocked public land and roads. Gangs sneaked out at night and cut the fences. At least three people were killed in fights between the fence cutters and ranchers. In January 1884, Texas lawmakers passed laws against fence-cutting and made the punishment one to five years in prison.

END OF THE COWBOY ERA

By 1885, more than 400,000 settlers had moved west. Many settled in Texas and Kansas. By 1889, part of Indian Territory was open to the settlers. These newcomers fenced in their farmland and kept out the cattle drives. The end of the cowboy era was near.

The U.S. government encouraged people to move to the wide-open land in the Great Plains. In 1862, the Homestead Act offered 160 acres (65 hectares) of free land to anyone who agreed to use the land for five years. The railroads also encouraged people to move west. As railroad companies laid tracks farther west, they advertised the good land and fresh air. The trains brought farmers and ranchers, who put up more fences. The days of wide-open cattle ranges came to an end.

Month by month the railroads built farther west and south. By 1890, trains rolled right into central Texas. There was no longer any need for cowboys to walk the cattle to cow towns in Kansas.

Indian Territory

By 1887, land in Indian Territory started to look attractive to settlers. In a series of agreements and laws, the U.S. government took land away from the Creek, Seminole, Cheyenne, Arapaho, Cherokee, and other tribes. The government encouraged American Indians to take small areas of land to farm. The rest of the land was open to settlers. In 1890, the Indian Territory had 179,321 people. Only 50,000 were American Indians. The rest were settlers. The territory eventually became Oklahoma.

ANNIE OAKLEY
Annie Oakley joined Buffalo Bill's *Wild West Show* in an act called "Little Sure Shot". She could shoot a hole through a playing card tossed in the air from 90 feet (27 meters) away.

▶ These cowboys of the 1890s are fixing fences at the edge of the ranch's pasture. Today there are hundreds of cattle ranches in the Southwest. Cowboys do many of the same jobs they did in the 1870s, such as branding cattle and taking care of horses. Modern cowboys ride the range in pickup trucks and search for stray cattle from helicopters.

▶ In 1883, Buffalo Bill Cody started his traveling *Wild West Show*. He brought cowboys, cowgirls, and American Indians to towns around the nation and to Europe. This poster from 1890 advertises Buffalo Bill's show.

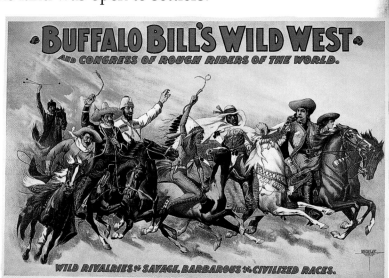

BUFFALO BILL'S WILD WEST
AND CONGRESS OF ROUGH RIDERS OF THE WORLD.

WILD RIVALRIES OF SAVAGE, BARBAROUS AND CIVILIZED RACES.

CHANGES

About 30,000 cowboys and 10 million cattle walked the cattle drives from 1865 to 1890. Here are reasons why cattle drives ended:
• Ranchers and farmers moved to the cattle drive areas.
• Barbed-wire fences closed off the range.
• Railroad tracks reached Texas. As a result, cowboys led cattle from a fenced-in area to a railroad just a few miles away.

Cowboys live on

Some cowboys joined exciting traveling shows and entertained U.S. citizens with broncobusting and sharpshooting. For the next century, stage plays, movies, books, and TV shows kept the cowboys alive. Audiences learned about the tough, daring side of cowboy heroes. The dirty, boring, frightening side was left out.

HISTORICAL MAP OF THE UNITED STATES

In 1880, the United States had 38 states and 9 territories. Cattle drives followed trails from Texas to towns in Colorado, Wyoming, and Montana, where the cattle were used to feed miners, railroad workers, and American Indians on reservations. Other cattle drives went to Kansas and Nebraska on the Chisholm, Western, and Shawnee trails. These drives ended in cow towns located by the railroad.

River
Railroad
Goodnight–Loving Trail
Western Trail
Shawnee/Sedalia Trail
Chisholm Trail
Texas–Abilene Trail
Indian reservations in 1880

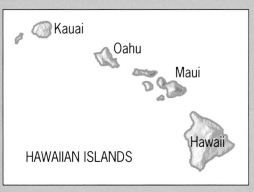

0   250   500 miles
0   400   800 kilometers

Hudson Bay

CANADA

Lake Superior

MINNESOTA

NORTH
DAKOTA

WISCONSIN

SOUTH
DAKOTA

Minneapolis

Milwaukee

Lake Huron

Lake Michigan

MICHIGAN

Detroit

Lake
Ontario

NEW YORK

St. Lawrence

MAINE

VERMONT

NEW HAMPSHIRE

MASSACHUSETTS
Boston

RHODE ISLAND

CONNECTICUT

New York City

NEW JERSEY

Philadelphia

DELAWARE

MARYLAND

Washington, D.C.

ATLANTIC OCEAN

Chicago

IOWA

Mississippi River

NEBRASKA

Kansas
City

KANSAS

Abilene

Dodge
City

Topeka

Sedalia

MISSOURI

St. Louis

ILLINOIS

INDIANA

OHIO

Cleveland

Pittsburgh

Lake Erie

PENNSYLVANIA

Delaware River

Hudson River

WEST
VIRGINIA

VIRGINIA

Ohio River

KENTUCKY

James
River

NORTH
CAROLINA

APPALACHIAN MOUNTAINS

OKLAHOMA

ARKANSAS

TENNESSEE

Memphis

Mississippi River

SOUTH
CAROLINA

Charleston

Birmingham

Atlanta

GEORGIA

Savannah

Fort
Worth

Dallas

MISSISSIPPI

ALABAMA

LOUISIANA

Jacksonville

TEXAS

Houston

New Orleans

FLORIDA

San Antonio

Rio Grande River

GULF OF MEXICO

Missouri
River

CARIBBEAN SEA

GLOSSARY

barbed wire metal wire, used for fences, that has sharp points on it

boardinghouse place to live where meals are provided

border line that separates one country, state, or region from another

brand mark burned into the hide of a cow to show who owns it

breed produce young animals (or plants), particularly to get a new or improved kind

broncobuster person who tames wild horses so that people can ride them

bunkhouse building on the ranch where cowboys sleep

cattle drive long journey to walk cattle from a ranch to a place where they are sold

chaps long pieces of wool or leather worn over a cowboy's pants to protect the legs

chuckwagon wagon taken on cattle drives in which a cook prepares meals for the cowboys

Civil War (1861 to 1865) in the United States, a war between the North and the South

cow town town on a cattle drive where cows were put onto trains

deadline in the 1800s, a line marked in the ground by farmers that cattle were not supposed to cross

demand desire and ability to buy

gambling play games for money. The games involve taking a risk.

gold rush starting in 1849, the time when many people went to California to find gold

hide animal skin. Leather is made from the hides of cattle.

lariat long rope used for catching horses and cattle

line camp shack far out on the range where cowboys stayed to watch the cattle

marshal law officer in charge of a town

mess hall place on the ranch where cowboys ate

plains wide area of flat or gently rolling land. The Great Plains is land between the Mississippi River and the Rocky Mountains.

ranch farm where cattle, horses, or sheep are raised. The person who owns the ranch is called a rancher.

range area of open land used for a particular purpose

reservation area of land set aside by the U.S. government for American Indians to live

roundup gathering of cattle for branding or taking on a cattle drive

rustler cattle or horse thief

saloon place where alcoholic drinks are sold

slave someone who is owned by another person and is made to work for that person without pay

stampede sudden scattering of cattle when they become frightened

tallow fat from sheep or cows that is melted

and used to make candles, soap, and other products

territory in the United States, an area that was not yet a state. Indian Territory was land set aside (in present-day Oklahoma) by the government for American Indians. But settlers were able to move onto American Indian land.

trader person who purchases things by exchanging one kind of good for another. Traders traveled from one place to another to exchange goods.

trail boss person in charge of the cattle drive

vaquero in Spain and Mexico, worker who took care of the cattle. *Vaca* is the Spanish word for "cow."

wrangler person who takes care of the horses on a ranch or cattle drive

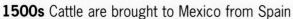

TIMELINE OF EVENTS IN THIS BOOK

1500s Cattle are brought to Mexico from Spain

1700s Cattle spread from Mexico to Texas

1821 Mexico wins independence from Spain, and Texas becomes part of Mexico

1835 The U.S. government starts sending American Indians to Indian Territory from places east of the Mississippi River

1836 Texas wins independence from Mexico

1845 Texas joins the United States

1848 Gold is discovered near Sacramento, California. From Mexico the United States gains the following territories: present-day California, Nevada and Utah, plus parts of Wyoming, New Mexico, Colorado, and Arizona.

1849 to 1854 Main years of the California gold rush

1854 The Chicago and Rock Island Railroad is the first train to reach the Mississippi River from the East

1861 to 1865 The North and the South fight the Civil War

1862 Homestead Act offers free land in the West

1863 to 1869 The Union Pacific and Central Pacific Railroads build the first railroad across the United States between the Atlantic and Pacific Coasts

1866 Oliver Loving and Charles Goodnight start selling cattle in New Mexico. The Goodnight–Loving Trail is named after them.

1867 Joseph McCoy starts to build the cow town of Abilene, Kansas. Chisholm Trail cattle drives begin.

1871 Wild Bill Hickok becomes marshal of Abilene

1872 Citizens of Abilene stop cattle drives from coming into town

1873 Joseph Glidden develops barbed wire

1875 to 1885 Dodge City is the last and busiest cow town

1883 Buffalo Bill Cody starts his traveling *Wild West Show*

1884 Texas lawmakers make fence-cutting illegal

1885 Cattle drives on the Chisholm Trail end

1886 to 1887 A deadly winter kills hundreds of thousands of cattle

1889 Land in Indian Territory is opened for settlers, and the first land rush in Oklahoma takes place. The U.S. government allows settlers to claim land that had been formerly given to American Indians.

1890 Trains are built to central Texas

FURTHER READING

Freedman, Russell. *In the Days of the Vaqueros: America's First True Cowboys.* Boston, Mass.: Houghton Mifflin, 2001.

Hominick, Judy, and Jeanne Spreier. *Best Cowboy in the West: The Story of Nat Love.* New York: Silver Moon Press, 2001.

McCall, Edith. *Adventures of Cowboys on Cattle Drives, Volume 5.* Unionville, N.Y.: Royal Fireworks Publishing, 2001.

Sanford, William R. *The Chisholm Trail in American History.* Berkeley Heights, N.J.: Enslow Publishers, 2000.

Schlissel, Lillian. *Black Frontiers: A History of African American Heroes in the Old West.* New York: Simon and Schuster, 2000.

Sundling, Charles W. *Cowboys of the Frontier.* Edina, Minn.: ABDO Publishing, 2000.

Vigil, Angel. *Riding Tall in the Saddle: The Cowboy Fact Book.* Englewood, Col.: Libraries Unlimited, 2002.

Woog, Adam. *A Cowboy in the Old West.* Farmington Hills, Mich.: The Gale Group, 2002.

Worcester, Donald E. *Cowboy with a Camera: Erwin E. Smith, Cowboy Photographer.* Fort Worth, Tex.: Amon Carter Museum, 1999.

PLACES TO VISIT

Chisholm Trail Heritage Center
1000 N. 29th Street
Duncan, OK 73534
Telephone: (580) 252-6692

Dickinson County Heritage Center
412 South Campbell
Abilene, KS 67410
Telephone: (785) 263-2681

Boot Hill Museum
Front Street
Dodge City, KS 67801
Telephone: (620) 227-8188

Old Cow Town Museum
1871 Sim Park Dr.
Wichita, KS 67203
Telephone: (316) 264-0671

Gene Autry Oklahoma Museum
P.O. Box 67
Gene Autry, OK 73436
Telephone: (580) 294-3047

INDEX